Interactive Notebooks

LANGUAGE ARTS

Kindergarten

Credits

Content Editor: Angela Triplett

Visit *carsondellosa.com* for correlations to Common Core, state, national, and Canadian provincial standards.

Carson-Dellosa Publishing, LLC
PO Box 35665
Greensboro, NC 27425 USA
carsondellosa.com

978-1-4838-2467-3
02-191157784

Table of Contents

© Carson-Dellosa • CD-104651

What Are Interactive Notebooks?

Interactive notebooks are a unique form of note taking. Teachers guide students through creating pages of notes on new topics. Instead of being in the traditional linear, handwritten format, notes are colorful and spread across the pages. Notes also often include drawings, diagrams, and 3-D elements to make the material understandable and relevant. Students are encouraged to complete their notebook pages in ways that make sense to them. With this personalization, no two pages are exactly the same.

Because of their creative nature, interactive notebooks allow students to be active participants in their own learning. Teachers can easily differentiate pages to address the levels and needs of each learner. The notebooks are arranged sequentially, and students can create tables of contents as they create pages, making it simple for students to use their notebooks for reference throughout the year. The interactive, easily personalized format makes interactive notebooks ideal for engaging students in learning new concepts.

Using interactive notebooks can take as much or as little time as you like. Students will initially take longer to create pages but will get faster as they become familiar with the process of creating pages. You may choose to only create a notebook page as a class at the beginning of each unit, or you may choose to create a new page for each topic within a unit. You can decide what works best for your students and schedule.

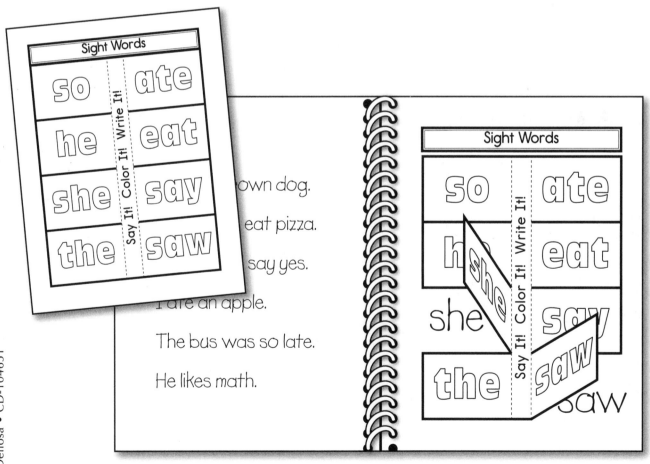

A student's interactive notebook for sight words

Getting Started

You can start using interactive notebooks at any point in the school year. Use the following guidelines to help you get started in your classroom. (For more specific details, management ideas, and tips, see page 10.)

1. Plan each notebook.

Use the planning template (page 9) to lay out a general plan for the topics you plan to cover in each notebook for the year.

2. Choose a notebook type.

Interactive notebooks are usually either single-subject, spiral-bound notebooks; composition books; or three-ring binders with loose-leaf paper. Each type presents pros and cons. See page 5 for a more in-depth look at each type of notebook.

3. Allow students to personalize their notebooks.

Have students decorate their notebook covers, as well as add their names and subjects. This provides a sense of ownership and emphasizes the personalized nature of the notebooks.

4. Number the pages and create the table of contents.

Have students number the bottom outside corner of each page, front and back. When completing a new page, adding a table of contents entry will be easy. Have students title the first page of each notebook "Table of Contents." Have them leave several blank pages at the front of each notebook for the table of contents. Refer to your general plan for an idea of about how many entries students will be creating.

5. Start creating pages.

Always begin a new page by adding an entry to the table of contents. Create the first notebook pages along with students to model proper format and expectations.

This book contains individual topics for you to introduce. Use the pages in the order that best fits your curriculum. You may also choose to alter the content presented to better match your school's curriculum. The provided lesson plans often do not instruct students to add color. Students should make their own choices about personalizing the content in ways that make sense to them. Encourage students to highlight and color the pages as they desire while creating them.

After introducing topics, you may choose to add more practice pages. Use the reproducibles (pages 78–96) to easily create new notebook pages for practice or to introduce topics not addressed in this book.

Use the grading rubric (page 11) to grade students' interactive notebooks at various points throughout the year. Provide students with copies of the rubric to glue into their notebooks and refer to as they create pages.

What Type of Notebook Should I Use?

Spiral Notebook

The pages in this book are formatted for a standard one-subject notebook.

Pros

- Notebook can be folded in half.
- Page size is larger.
- It is inexpensive.
- It often comes with pockets for storing materials.

Cons

- Pages can easily fall out.
- Spirals can snag or become misshapen.
- Page count and size vary widely.
- It is not as durable as a binder.

Tips

- Encase the spiral in duct tape to make it more durable.
- Keep the notebooks in a central place to prevent them from getting damaged in desks.

Composition Notebook

Pros

- Pages don't easily fall out.
- Page size and page count are standard.
- It is inexpensive.

Cons

- Notebook cannot be folded in half.
- Page size is smaller.
- It is not as durable as a binder.

Tips

- Copy pages meant for standard-sized notebooks at 85 or 90 percent. Test to see which works better for your notebook.

Binder with Loose-Leaf Paper

Pros

- Pages can be easily added, moved, or removed.
- Pages can be removed individually for grading.
- You can add full-page printed handouts.
- It has durable covers.

Cons

- Pages can easily fall out.
- Pages aren't durable.
- It is more expensive than a notebook.
- Students can easily misplace or lose pages.
- Larger size makes it more difficult to store.

Tips

- Provide hole reinforcers for damaged pages.

How to Organize an Interactive Notebook

You may organize an interactive notebook in many different ways. You may choose to organize it by unit and work sequentially through the book. Or, you may choose to create different sections that you will revisit and add to throughout the year. Choose the format that works best for your students and subject.

An interactive notebook includes different types of pages in addition to the pages students create. Non-content pages you may want to add include the following:

Title Page

This page is useful for quickly identifying notebooks. It is especially helpful in classrooms that use multiple interactive notebooks for different subjects. Have students write the subject (such as "Language Arts") on the title page of each interactive notebook. They should also include their full names. You may choose to have them include other information such as the teacher's name, classroom number, or class period.

Table of Contents

The table of contents is an integral part of the interactive notebook. It makes referencing previously created pages quick and easy for students. Make sure that students leave several pages at the beginning of each notebook for a table of contents.

Expectations and Grading Rubric

It is helpful for each student to have a copy of the expectations for creating interactive notebook pages. You may choose to include a list of expectations for parents and students to sign, as well as a grading rubric (page 11).

Unit Title Pages

Consider using a single page at the beginning of each section to separate it. Title the page with the unit name. Add a tab (page 78) to the edge of the page to make it easy to flip to the unit. Add a table of contents for only the pages in that unit.

Glossary

Reserve a six-page section at the back of the notebook where students can create a glossary. Draw a line to split in half the front and back of each page, creating 24 sections. Combine Q and R and Y and Z to fit the entire alphabet. Have students add an entry as each new vocabulary word is introduced.

Formatting Student Notebook Pages

The other major consideration for planning an interactive notebook is how to treat the left and right sides of a notebook spread. Interactive journals are usually viewed with the notebook open flat. This creates a left side and a right side. You have several options for how to treat the two sides of the spread.

Traditionally, the right side is used for the teacher-directed part of the lesson, and the left side is used for students to interact with the lesson content. The lessons in this book use this format. However, you may prefer to switch the order for your class so that the teacher-directed learning is on the left and the student input is on the right.

It can also be important to include standards, learning objectives, or essential questions in interactive notebooks. You may choose to write these on the top-left side of each page before completing the teacher-directed page on the right side. You may also choose to have students include the "Introduction" part of each lesson in that same top-left section. This is the *in, through, out* method. Students enter *in* the lesson on the top left of the page, go *through* the lesson on the right page, and exit *out* of the lesson on the bottom left with a reflection activity.

The following chart details different types of items and activities that you could include on each side.

Left Side Student Output	Right Side Teacher-Directed Learning
• learning objectives • essential questions • I Can statements • brainstorming • making connections • summarizing • making conclusions • practice problems • opinions • questions • mnemonics • drawings and diagrams	• vocabulary and definitions • mini-lessons • folding activities • steps in a process • example problems • notes • diagrams • graphic organizers • hints and tips • big ideas

Planning for the Year

Making a general plan for interactive notebooks will help with planning, grading, and testing throughout the year. You do not need to plan every single page, but knowing what topics you will cover and in what order can be helpful in many ways.

Use the Interactive Notebook Plan (page 9) to plan your units and topics and where they should be placed in the notebooks. Remember to include enough pages at the beginning for the non-content pages, such as the title page, table of contents, and grading rubric. You may also want to leave a page at the beginning of each unit to place a mini table of contents for just that section.

In addition, when planning new pages, it can be helpful to sketch the pieces you will need to create. Use the following notebook template and notes to plan new pages.

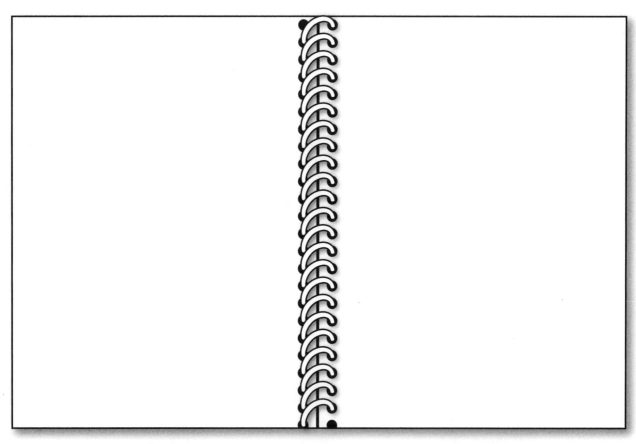

Left Side   **Right Side**

Notes

_____

_____

_____

Interactive Notebook Plan

Page	Topic	Page	Topic
1		51	
2		52	
3		53	
4		54	
5		55	
6		56	
7		57	
8		58	
9		59	
10		60	
11		61	
12		62	
13		63	
14		64	
15		65	
16		66	
17		67	
18		68	
19		69	
20		70	
21		71	
22		72	
23		73	
24		74	
25		75	
26		76	
27		77	
28		78	
29		79	
30		80	
31		81	
32		82	
33		83	
34		84	
35		85	
36		86	
37		87	
38		88	
39		89	
40		90	
41		91	
42		92	
43		93	
44		94	
45		95	
46		96	
47		97	
48		98	
49		99	
50		100	

Managing Interactive Notebooks in the Classroom

Working with Younger Students

- Use your yearly plan to preprogram a table of contents that you can copy and give to students to glue into their notebooks, instead of writing individual entries.

- Have assistants or parent volunteers precut pieces.

- Create glue sponges to make gluing easier. Place large sponges in plastic containers with white glue. The sponges will absorb the glue. Students can wipe the backs of pieces across the sponges to apply the glue with less mess.

Creating Notebook Pages

- For storing loose pieces, add a pocket to the inside back cover. Use the envelope pattern (page 81), an envelope, or a resealable plastic bag. Or, tape the bottom and side edges of the two last pages of the notebook together to create a large pocket.

- When writing under flaps, have students trace the outline of each flap so that they can visualize the writing boundary.

- Where the dashed line will be hidden on the inside of the fold, have students first fold the piece in the opposite direction so that they can see the dashed line. Then, students should fold the piece back the other way along the same fold line to create the fold in the correct direction.

- To avoid losing pieces, have students keep all of their scraps on their desks until they have finished each page.

- To contain paper scraps and avoid multiple trips to the trash can, provide small groups with small buckets or tubs.

- For students who run out of room, keep full and half sheets available. Students can glue these to the bottom of the pages and fold them up when not in use.

Dealing with Absences

- Create a model notebook for absent students to reference when they return to school.

- Have students cut a second set of pieces as they work on their own pages.

Using the Notebook

- To organize sections of the notebook, provide each student with a sheet of tabs (page 78).

- To easily find the next blank page, either cut off the top-right corner of each page as it is used or attach a long piece of yarn or ribbon to the back cover to be used as a bookmark.

Interactive Notebook Grading Rubric

4

_____ Table of contents is complete.

_____ All notebook pages are included.

_____ All notebook pages are complete.

_____ Notebook pages are neat and organized.

_____ Information is correct.

_____ Pages show personalization, evidence of learning, and original ideas.

3

_____ Table of contents is mostly complete.

_____ One notebook page is missing.

_____ Notebook pages are mostly complete.

_____ Notebook pages are mostly neat and organized.

_____ Information is mostly correct.

_____ Pages show some personalization, evidence of learning, and original ideas.

2

_____ Table of contents is missing a few entries.

_____ A few notebook pages are missing.

_____ A few notebook pages are incomplete.

_____ Notebook pages are somewhat messy and unorganized.

_____ Information has several errors.

_____ Pages show little personalization, evidence of learning, or original ideas.

1

_____ Table of contents is incomplete.

_____ Many notebook pages are missing.

_____ Many notebook pages are incomplete.

_____ Notebook pages are too messy and unorganized to use.

_____ Information is incorrect.

_____ Pages show no personalization, evidence of learning, or original ideas.

Uppercase Letters: A-Z

This lesson is designed to introduce one or more letters at a time and can be taught over several days. The letters can be glued onto several pages of the notebook.

Introduction

Display or write the uppercase letter *A* on the board. Introduce students to the letter's sound by singing a song or reading a poem that repeats the sound. Ask students to provide examples of words that begin with the letter. Demonstrate how to properly write the uppercase letter. Repeat the activity with each letter of the alphabet.

Creating the Notebook Page

Guide students through the following steps to complete the right-hand page in their notebooks.

1. Add a Table of Contents entry for the Uppercase Letters: *A–Z* pages.

2. Cut out the title and glue it to the top of the page.

3. Trace each letter using your finger. Then, trace each letter with a pencil.

4. Cut out each letter and glue it to the left side of the page.

5. Practice writing each letter several times. Then, draw a picture of something that starts with each letter.

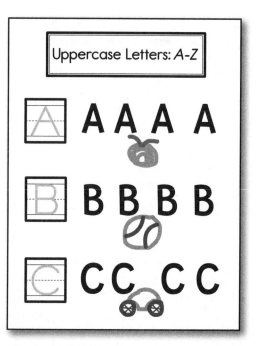

Reflect on Learning

To complete the left-hand page, students should write the letter or letters that were introduced in the lesson along the left side of the page. Provide students with magazines and newspapers. Have students find and cut out examples of the letter or letters and glue the examples beside the correct letters.

© Carson-Dellosa • CD-104651

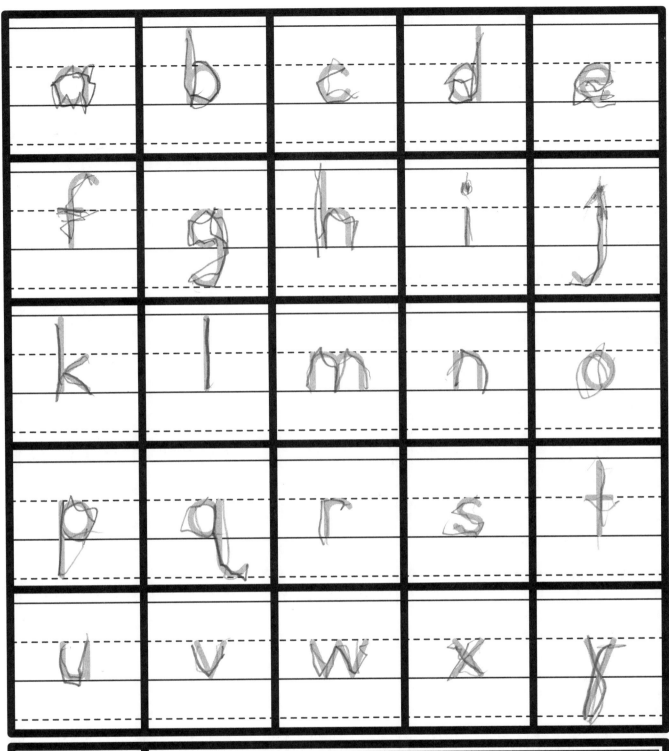

Lowercase Letters: a-z

Matching Uppercase and Lowercase Letters

For each letter, review the sound or sounds that the letter makes. Ask students to read around the classroom and provide examples with words that contain the letter. Write or display the uppercase letter. Then, write or display the lowercase letter beside it. Compare the uppercase letter with the lowercase letter. Encourage students to find similarities and differences between the letters.

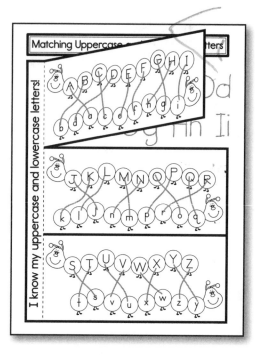

Creating the Notebook Page

Guide students through the following steps to complete the right-hand page in their notebooks.

1. Add a Table of Contents entry for the Matching Uppercase and Lowercase Letters pages.

2. Cut out the title and glue it to the top of the page.

3. Cut out the flap book. Cut on the solid lines to create three flaps. Apply glue to the back of the left section and attach it to the page.

4. On each flap, draw a line to match each uppercase letter to the correct lowercase letter.

5. Practice writing the uppercase and lowercase letters under each flap.

Reflect on Learning

To complete the left-hand page, students should choose five uppercase letters. Students should use markers to write them along the left side of the page. Using a different color, they should write the matching lowercase letters along the right side of the page.

Vowel Sounds: Short a

Vowel Sounds: Short *e*

Students will need a sharpened pencil and a paper clip to complete the spinner activity.

Introduction

Review the short *e* sound. Read a poem or a short story that repeats words that have the short *e* sound. Have students to share short *e* words they heard in the poem or story. Write the words on the board. Have volunteers come to the board, say the words, and circle the short *e* sound in each word.

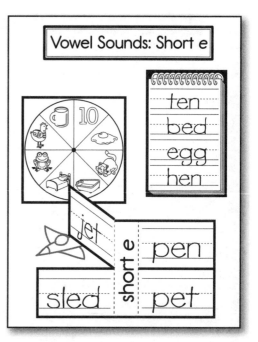

Creating the Notebook Page

Guide students through the following steps to complete the right-hand page in their notebooks.

1. Add a Table of Contents entry for the Vowel Sounds: Short *e* pages.

2. Cut out the title and glue it to the top of the page.

3. Cut out the spinner and glue it to the top left side of the page. Then, cut out the notepad and glue it beside the spinner.

4. Use a sharpened pencil and a paper clip to spin the spinner. If the spinner lands on a short *e* word, write the word on the notepad. Spin until the notepad is filled with four short *e* words.

5. Cut out the *short e* flap book. Cut on the solid lines to create two flaps on each side. Apply glue to the back of the title section and attach it to the bottom of the page.

6. Write a short *e* word on each flap. Highlight the short *e* sound.

7. Draw a picture for the word under each flap.

Reflect on Learning

To complete the left-hand page, each student should draw a five-circle bubble map with the middle circle labeled *short e*. Students should write or draw one short *e* word in each of the other circles.

Vowel Sounds: Short e

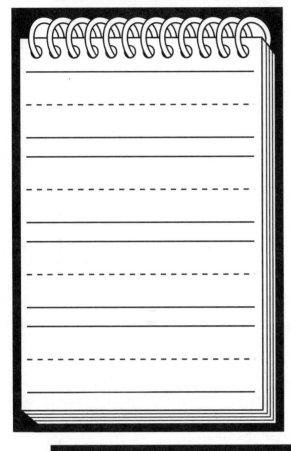

short e

Vowel Sounds: Short *i*

Review the short *i* sound. Read a poem or a short story that repeats words with the short *i* sound. Each time you read a short *i* word, have students clap their hands. List a few words from the poem or short story on the board. Have volunteers come to the board, say the words, and circle the short *i* sound in each word.

Creating the Notebook Page

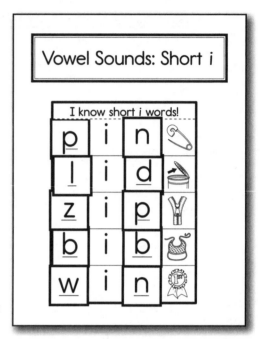

Guide students through the following steps to complete the right-hand page in their notebooks.

1. Add a Table of Contents entry for the Vowel Sounds: Short *i* pages.

2. Cut out the title and glue it to the top of the page.

3. Cut out the *I know short i words!* flap. Apply glue to the back of the top section and attach it to the page.

4. Cut out the letters.

5. Complete the words on the card by placing the beginning and ending letters in the correct boxes beside the picture. Glue the letters when all of the words are spelled correctly.

6. Practice writing or drawing pictures of short *i* words under the flap.

Reflect on Learning

To complete the left-hand page, have students write *Short i* at the top of the page. Provide students with magazines and newspapers. Have students cut out pictures of objects with names that contain the short *i* sound and glue them onto the page.

b	l	z	w	p
p	n	d	b	n

I know short *i* words!

	i		
	i		
	i		
	i		
	i		

Vowel Sounds: Short *i*

Vowel Sounds: Short *o*

Introduction

Review the short *o* sound. Read a poem or a short story that contains words with the short *o* sound. Then, have students stand in a circle. Pass a small ball around the circle as you play music. Stop the music intermittently. The student holding the ball should say a word that has the short *o* sound in it. If he cannot think of a word, or says a word that has been used, he must sit down. Continue the activity until only one student is left standing.

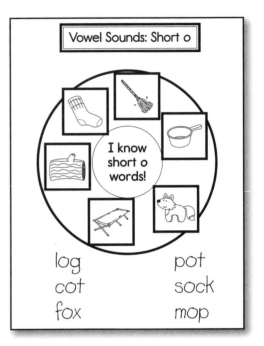

Creating the Notebook Page

Guide students through the following steps to complete the right-hand page in their notebooks.

1. Add a Table of Contents entry for the Vowel Sounds: Short *o* pages.

2. Cut out the title and glue it to the top of the page.

3. Cut out the circle map and glue it below the title.

4. Cut out the picture cards. Say the name of each picture. Then, glue each picture onto the circle map.

5. Write the name of each picture under the circle map.

Reflect on Learning

To complete the left-hand page, have students draw a circle map. Then, write *Short o* in the middle of the circle and write or draw pictures of more short *o* words in the circle map.

I know short o words!

Vowel Sounds: Short o

Vowel Sounds: Short *u*

Introduction

Review the short *u* sound. Program and display index cards with the letters *b, h, g, m, t,* and *u*. Show a picture of a mug. As a class, use the letter cards to sound out and build the word *mug*. Write the word on the board. Replace the letter cards. Show a picture of a hut. Have a volunteer to come to the board and use the letter cards to build the word *hut*. Then, write the word on the board. Repeat the activity with a picture of a tub.

Creating the Notebook Page

Guide students through the following steps to complete the right-hand page in their notebooks.

1. Add a Table of Contents entry for the Vowel Sounds: Short *u* pages.

2. Cut out the title and glue it to the top of the page.

3. Cut out each flap. Apply glue to the back of the top section and attach each flap to the page.

4. Under each flap, use the letters shown to write the name of the picture on the flap. Highlight the short *u* sound in each word.

Reflect on Learning

To complete the left-hand page, write the following words on the board: *cut, run, fun, dug, hug*. Have students copy the words and highlight the short *u* sound in each word.

b g u

n s u

j g u

t n u

p c u

u r g

Vowel Sounds: Short *u*

Short and Long Vowel Sounds

Introduction

Introduction

Review short and long vowel sounds. Have students look around the room for objects with names that have short vowel sounds such as *desk*, *pen*, and *flag*. Then, have students name body parts that contain a long vowel sound such as *nose*, *feet*, and *knees*. Next, play a vowel sound game. Explain that you will say a word. If the word has a short vowel sound, students should squeeze their hands. If the word contains a long vowel sound, students should stretch their hands to each side. Say various short and long vowel sound words to allow students to practice hearing the vowel sound in each word.

Creating the Notebook Page

Guide students through the following steps to complete the right-hand page in their notebooks.

1. Add a Table of Contents entry for the Short and Long Vowel Sounds pages.

2. Cut out the title and glue it to the top of the page.

3. Cut out the *Short Vowels* and *Long Vowels* labels and glue them below the title to form two columns.

4. Cut out the picture cards. Say the name of each picture. Sort and glue each picture below the correct label.

Reflect on Learning

To complete the left-hand page, have each student draw a T-chart labeled *Short* and *Long*. Provide students with magazines and newspapers. Have students cut out pictures of objects with names that have the short and long vowel sounds and glue them into the correct columns.

Short and Long Vowel Sounds

Short Vowels | Long Vowels

Word Families: -ad, -an, -at

This lesson is designed to introduce one or more word families at a time and can be taught over several days.

Introduction

Review the sound each word family makes. Have students brainstorm a list of words that belong in each word family. Write the words on the board. Ask students what they notice about the words. Possible answers may include that the words rhyme, they have one syllable, or that the words look the same except for the beginning sound. Have volunteers come to the board, circle the beginning sound (onset), and underline the word family (rime) in each word listed.

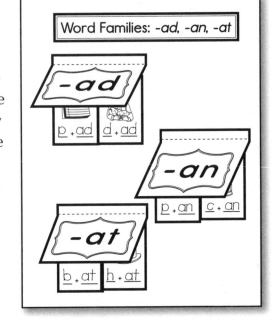

Creating the Notebook Page

Guide students through the following steps to complete the right-hand page in their notebooks.

1. Add a Table of Contents entry for the Word Families: *–ad, –an, –at* pages.

2. Cut out the title and glue it to the top of the page.

3. Cut out the word family flaps. Apply glue to the back of the top sections and attach them to the page.

4. Cut out the picture cards. Say the name of the picture on each card. Complete each card by filling in the blanks with the correct onset and the rime.

5. Glue each card under the correct flap.

Reflect on Learning

To complete the left-hand page, students should make a chart with three columns. Then, write *–ad, –an,* and *–at* at the top of the columns. Have students write two words under each word family. Students should write the onset in blue and the rime in red.

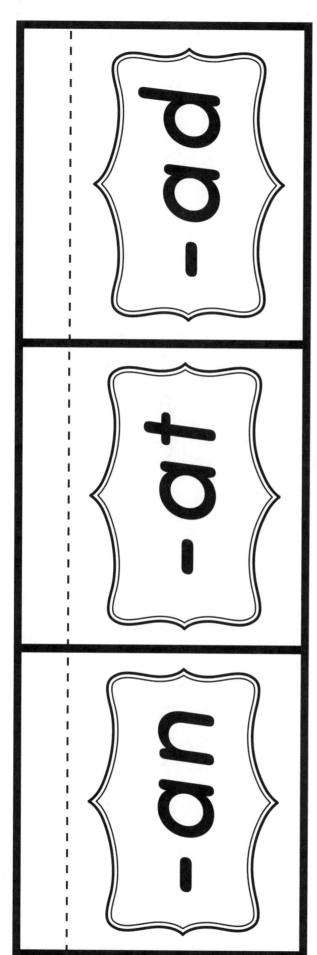

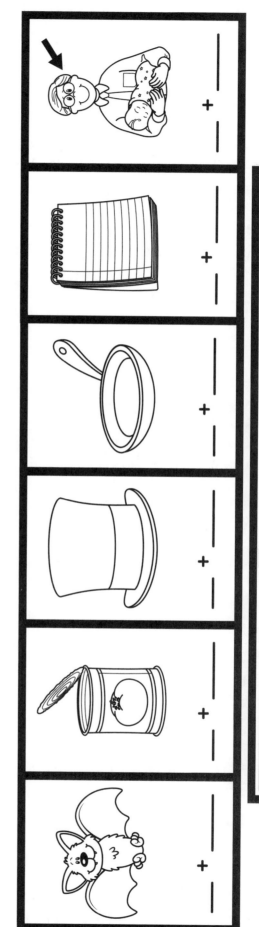

-ad

-at

-an

Word Families: -ad, -an, -at

Word Families: -ed, -en, -et

Students will need a sharpened pencil and a paper clip to complete the spinner activity. This lesson is designed to introduce one or more word families at a time and can be taught over several days.

Introduction

Review the sound each word family makes. Have students brainstorm a list of words that belong in each word family. Write the words on the board. Ask students what they notice about the words. Possible answers may include that the words rhyme, they have one syllable, or that the words look the same except for the beginning sound. Have volunteers come to the board, circle the beginning sound (onset), and underline the word family (rime) in each word listed.

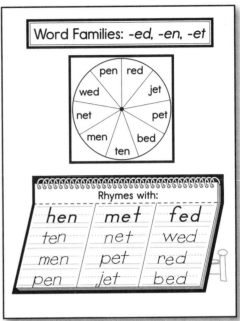

Creating the Notebook Page

Guide students through the following steps to complete the right-hand page in their notebooks.

1. Add a Table of Contents entry for the Word Families: *–ed, –en, –et* pages.

2. Cut out the title and glue it to the top of the page.

3. Cut out the spinner and glue it below the title.

4. Cut out the *Rhymes with:* flap. Apply glue to the back of the title section and attach it to the page below the spinner.

5. Use a sharpened pencil and a paper clip to spin the spinner. Say the word the spinner lands on. Write it in the correct column on the chart. Circle the onset in yellow and the rime in orange. Continue spinning until the chart is complete.

6. Draw lines under the flap to create three columns. Choose one word from each column and draw a picture of it under the flap.

Reflect on Learning

To complete the left-hand page, write this sentence on the board and read it aloud: *I wish I had ten red _____.* Ask students to copy the sentence into their notebooks, circle the short *e* words, and then fill in the blank. Then, students should draw a picture that illustrates the sentence.

Word Families: -ed, -en, -et

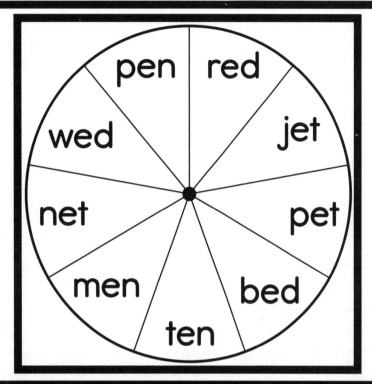

pen red wed jet net pet men bed ten

Rhymes with:

hen met fed

Word Families: -*ig, -in, -ip*

This lesson is designed to introduce one or more word families at a time and can be taught over several days.

Introduction

Review the sound each word family makes. Have students brainstorm a list of words that belong in each word family. Write the words on the board. Ask students what they notice about the words. Possible answers may include that the words rhyme, they have one syllable, or that the words look the same except for the beginning sound. Have volunteers come to the board, circle the beginning sound (onset), and underline the word family (rime) in each word listed.

Creating the Notebook Page

Guide students through the following steps to complete the right-hand page in their notebooks.

1. Add a Table of Contents entry for the Word Families: –*ig*, –*in*, –*ip* pages.

2. Cut out the title and glue it to the top of the page.

3. Cut out the letter pieces (onsets and rimes). Set aside.

4. Cut out the picture cards and glue them onto the page in three rows of two. Leave enough space to place two letter pieces below each picture. Glue the correct letter pieces to form the word under each picture card.

5. Color the beginning sound (onset) of each word piece with one color. Then, color the ending sounds (rime) with another.

Reflect on Learning

To complete the left-hand page, have students draw three large clouds. Then, write a word family in the middle of each cloud. Have students write three words below each word family and draw a raindrop around each word.

Word Families: *-ig, -in, -ip*

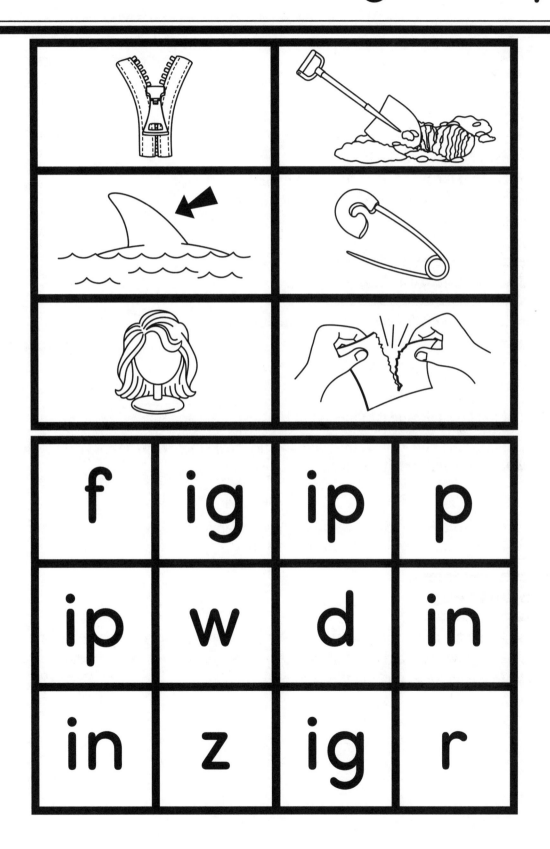

Word Families: -ob, -op, -ot

This lesson is designed to introduce one or more word families at a time and can be taught over several days.

Introduction

Review the sound each word family makes. Have students brainstorm a list of words that belong in each word family. Write the words on the board. Ask students what they notice about the words. Possible answers may include that the words rhyme, they have one syllable, or that the words look the same except for the beginning sound. Have volunteers come to the board, circle the beginning sound (onset, and underline the word family (rime) in each word listed.

Creating the Notebook Page

Guide students through the following steps to complete the right-hand page in their notebooks.

1. Add a Table of Contents entry for the Word Families: *–ob, –op, –ot* pages.

2. Cut out the title and glue it to the top of the page.

3. Cut out the flap book. Cut on the solid lines to create three flaps. Apply glue to the back of the left section and attach it to the page.

4. Cut out the strip of consonant letters. Glue the strip beside the flap book.

5. Cut out the word family cards. Move each word family card along the consonant strip until you make a word. Write it under the correct flap.

Reflect on Learning

To complete the left-hand page, students should glue the word family cards across the top of the page. Have students draw vertical lines to create three columns. Then, have students practice writing words from each word family in the columns.

Word Families: -ob, -op, -ot

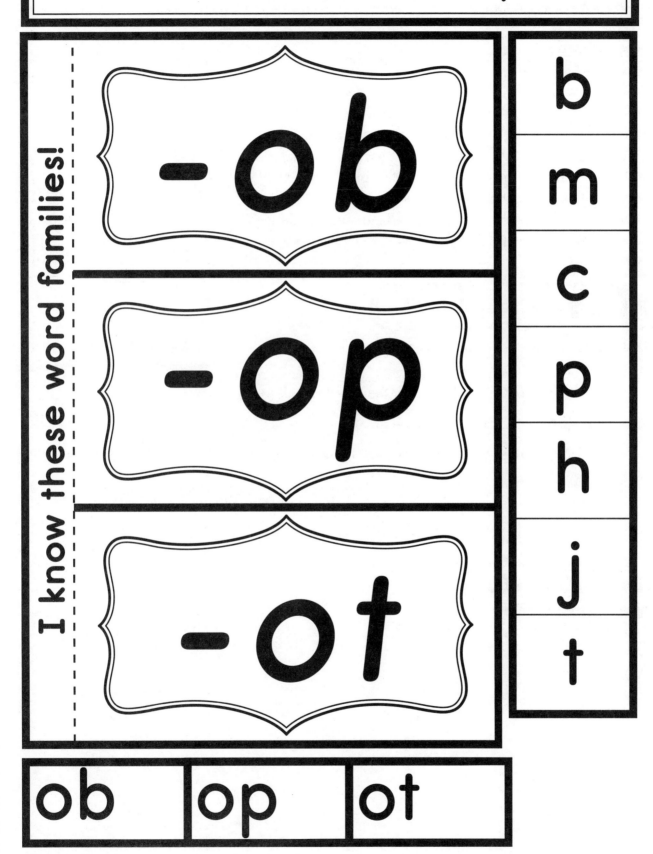

I know these word families!

-ob

-op

-ot

b
m
c
p
h
j
t

ob | op | ot

Word Families: -*ug*, -*un*, -*ut*

This lesson is designed to introduce one or more word families at a time and can be taught over several days.

Introduction

Review the sound each word family makes. Have students brainstorm a list of words that belong in each word family. Write the words on the board. Ask students what they notice about the words. Possible answers may include that the words rhyme, they have one syllable, or that the words look the same except for the beginning sound. Have volunteers come to the board, circle the beginning sound (onset), and underline the word family (rime) in each word listed.

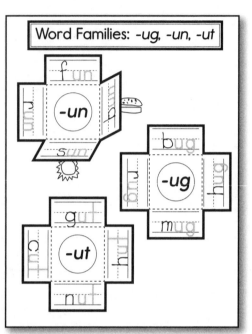

Creating the Notebook Page

Guide students through the following steps to complete the right-hand page in their notebooks.

1. Add a Table of Contents entry for the Word Families: –*ug*, –*un*, –*ut* pages.

2. Cut out the title and glue it to the top of the page.

3. Cut out each four-flap box. Apply glue to the back of the center sections and attach them to the page.

4. Write a letter of a beginning sound on each flap to complete the words.

5. Under each flap, draw a picture to represent the word.

Reflect on Learning

To complete the left-hand page, have students draw three large flowers. Then, have students write a word family in the center of each flower. Finally, students should write words from each word family on the flower petals.

Word Families: -ug, -un, -ut

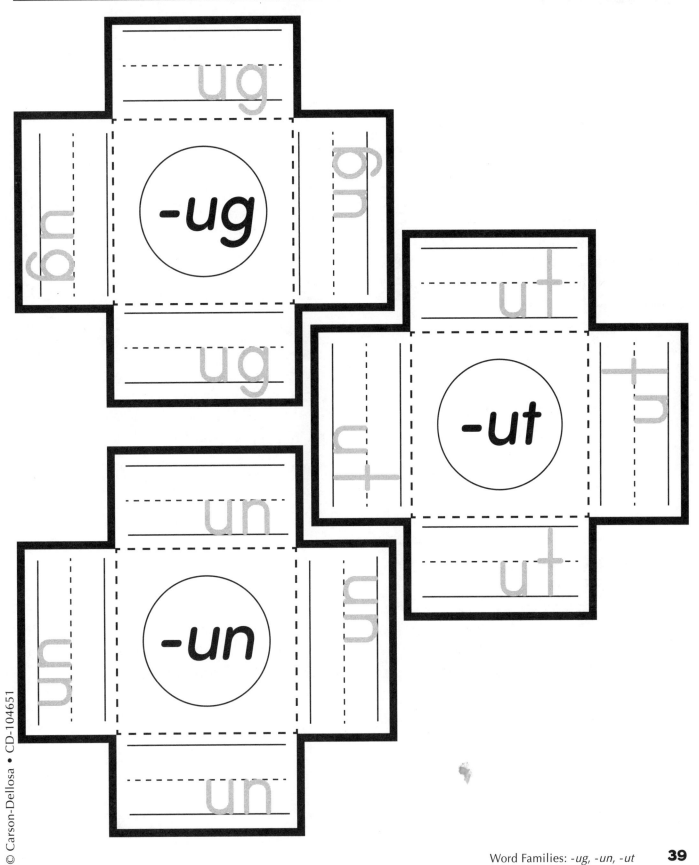

Sight Words: *all, am, be, get, like*

Students will need a sharpened pencil and a paper clip to complete the spinner activity.

Introduction

Explain that "sight words" are words that appear frequently in text. They are words that students will learn to read quickly just by looking at them. Review each sight word for this lesson. Write each word on the board. Then, draw a word shape box around each word and explain that recognizing the shape of a word can make it easier to read. am get

Sight Words

am get
like all
be

First place goes to ___get___ !
FINISH LINE

			get	
	be		get	
am	be	all	get	like
am	be	all	get	like
am	be	all	get	like

Creating the Notebook Page

Guide students through the following steps to complete the right-hand page in their notebooks.

1. Add a Table of Contents entry for the Sight Words: *all, am, be, get, like* pages.

2. Cut out the title and glue it to the top of the page.

3. Cut out the spinner and glue it below the title.

4. Cut out the sight word chart and glue it to the bottom of the page.

5. Use a sharpened pencil and a paper clip to spin the spinner. Write the word that the spinner lands on in the correct column of the chart beginning from the bottom.

6. The column completely filled first is the winner. Complete the sentence at the top of the chart by writing the winning word in the blank.

Reflect on Learning

To complete the left-hand page, have students write each sight word in large letters. Then, outline each one with a word shape box. Have them trace around each word shape box three times using a different color each time. For added practice, have students complete this activity using their names.

Sight Words

How Many Letters?

2 letters	3 letters	4 letters

I know these words!

Sight Words: *came, did, do, have, no, yes*

Introduction

Explain that "sight words" are words that appear frequently in text. They are words that students will learn to read quickly just by looking at them. Review each sight word for this lesson. Write each word on the board. Then, draw a word shape box around each word and explain that recognizing the shape of a word can make it easier to read.

Creating the Notebook Page

Guide students through the following steps to complete the right-hand page in their notebooks.

1. Add a Table of Contents entry for the Sight Words: *came, did, do, have, no, yes* pages.

2. Cut out the title and glue it to the top of the page.

3. Cut out the word bank and glue it below the title.

4. Cut out the fish pieces and glue them onto the page.

5. Use words from the word bank to fill in each word shape box.

Reflect on Learning

To complete the left-hand page, students should draw three columns and label them *Two Letters*, *Three Letters*, and *Four Letters*. They should write the correct sight words in each column. As a review, students can also write sight words they have learned previously in the correct columns.

Sight Words

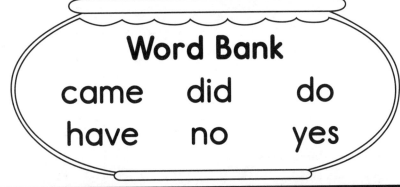

Word Bank

came   did   do

have   no   yes

Sight Words: *came, did, do, have, no, yes*

Nouns

Introduction

Introduce nouns by playing a simple game of I Spy with objects in the classroom. After the game, explain that the objects that were "spied" are nouns. Draw three columns on the board and label them *Person*, *Place*, and *Thing*. Then, call out a few more objects and have students decide if each noun is a person, place, or thing. Write each noun in the correct column.

Creating the Notebook Page

Guide students through the following steps to complete the right-hand page in their notebooks.

1. Add a Table of Contents entry for the Nouns pages.

2. Cut out the title and glue it to the top of the page.

3. Cut out the picture cards. Set them aside.

4. Cut out the flap book. Cut on the solid lines to create three flaps. Apply glue to the back of the left section and attach it to the page.

5. Glue each picture under the correct flap.

6. Write the name of or draw one more object under each flap.

Reflect on Learning

To complete the left-hand page, have students draw three columns and label them *People*, *Places*, and *Things*. Provide students with magazines and newspapers. Have students cut out pictures of objects that are nouns. Then, have students glue them in the correct columns.

Nouns

Person

Place

Thing

Nouns **49**

Verbs

Students will need a sharpened pencil and a paper clip to complete the spinner activity.

Introduction

To introduce verbs, play a game of Simon Says. Explain that every action that is performed is a verb. Verbs are words that describe doing something or a state of being. Reinforce this concept by having students act out emotions such as laughing, crying, or shouting. Then, read a short picture book. As you read, have students clap every time they hear a verb in the story.

Creating the Notebook Page

Guide students through the following steps to complete the right-hand page in their notebooks.

1. Add a Table of Contents entry for the Verbs pages.

2. Cut out the title and glue it to the top of the page.

3. Cut out the spinner and glue it below the title.

4. Use a sharpened pencil and a paper clip to spin the spinner. Say the verb the spinner lands on and act it out. Repeat the activity as time allows.

5. Cut out the flap book. Cut on the solid line to create two flaps. Apply glue to the back of the top section and attach it to the bottom of the page.

6. Draw a picture of a school and a home on the flaps. Then, write verbs or draw actions that are performed at school and at home under each flap.

Reflect on Learning

To complete the left-hand page, write this sentence on the board and read it aloud: *My cat plays with yarn.* Ask students to copy the sentence into their notebooks and circle the verb. Each student should draw a picture that illustrates the sentence.

Verbs

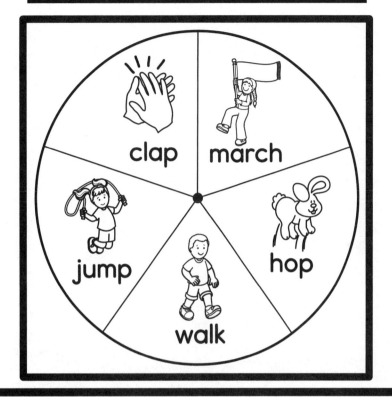

A **verb** is an action word.

Verbs at School

Verbs at Home

Plural Nouns

Introduction

To introduce plural nouns, draw a hat on the board. Write the word *hat* below the picture. Then, draw another hat beside the first. Add -*s* to the word. Tell students that when there is more than one of something, they should add -*s* to the word. Draw a box on the board. Write the word *box* below the picture. Draw another box beside the first. Add -*es* to the word. Ask students if they notice anything different this time. Explain that with a word that ends in -*ch*, -*sh*, -*s*, or -*x*, they should add -*es* to make it plural.

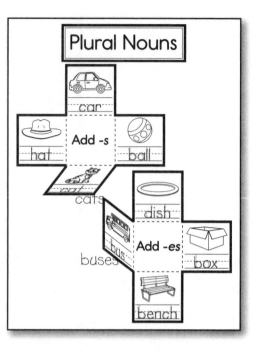

Creating the Notebook Page

Guide students through the following steps to complete the right-hand page in their notebooks.

1. Add a Table of Contents entry for the Plural Nouns pages.

2. Cut out the title and glue it to the top of the page.

3. Cut out the *Add -s* four-flap box. Apply glue to the back of the center section and attach it to the top-left side of the page.

4. Read and trace the word on each flap.

5. Write the plural form of each word under the flap.

6. Repeat steps 4 and 5 with the *Add -es* four-flap box.

Reflect on Learning

To complete the left-hand page, have each student draw a T-chart. Have students label one side with -*s* and the other side with -*es*. Students should write the plural words written under the flaps on each four-flap box in the correct columns.

Plural Nouns

Add -s

car

hat

ball

cat

Add -es

dish

bus

box

bench

Antonyms

Introduction

Explain that an antonym is a word that means the opposite of another word. Have students stand. Then, instruct students to sit. Tell students that they have just acted out an antonym word pair (*stand* and *sit*). Have two volunteers come to the front of the room. Quietly instruct one student to look "happy." Have the other student look "sad." Call on another student to tell the antonyms that describe each student. Encourage students to give more examples of opposite word pairs. Write a list on the board as the students give examples.

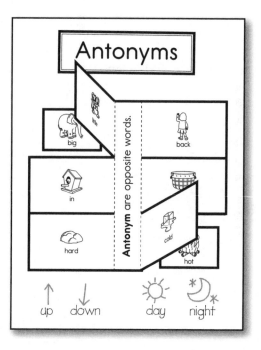

Creating the Notebook Page

Guide students through the following steps to complete the right-hand page in their notebooks.

1. Add a Table of Contents entry for the Antonyms pages.

2. Cut out the title and glue it to the top of the page.

3. Cut out the picture cards and set aside.

4. Cut out the flap book. Cut on the solid lines to create three flaps on each side. Apply glue to the back of the center section and attach it below the title.

5. Read each picture card and glue it under the correct flap.

6. Write two more opposite word pairs at the bottom of the page.

Reflect on Learning

To complete the left-hand page, provide students with magazines and newspapers. Write an opposite word pair on the board. Students should cut out pictures that show the meaning of each word in the word pair. For example, write *big* and *little* on the board. Students should find pictures that show an object that is big and an object that is little. Then, students should glue them onto the page and label each word.

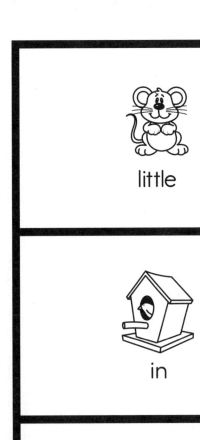

little

Antonyms are opposite words.

back

in

empty

hard

cold

front

out

full

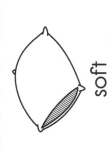

soft

hot

Antonyms

big

Sorting Objects

Introduction

Introduce categories as a way to put things in order. People can sort objects into categories. Say the following words: *sheep, cow, horse,* and *goat.* Ask students what the words have in common. Possible answers may include that the animals are farm animals or that they all have four legs. Say another list such as *shark, whale, fish,* and *camel.* Ask students which word does not belong. Discuss why *camel* does not belong.

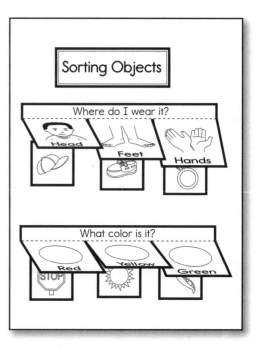

Creating the Notebook Page

Guide students through the following steps to complete the right-hand page in their notebooks.

1. Add a Table of Contents entry for the Sorting Objects pages.

2. Cut out the title and glue it to the top of the page.

3. Cut out the picture cards and set aside.

4. Cut out the *Where do I wear it?* flap book. Cut on the solid lines to create three flaps. Apply glue to the back of the top section and attach it to the top of the page.

5. Cut out the *What color is it?* flap book. Cut on the solid lines to create three flaps. Apply glue to the back of the top section and attach it to the bottom of the page. Color the circle on each flap with the correct color.

6. Sort and glue the pictures under the correct flaps.

Reflect on Learning

To complete the left-hand page, have each student draw a T-chart and label it *Water* and *Land.* Have students draw animals in the correct columns.

Where do I wear it?

	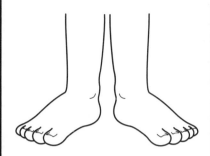	
Head	**Feet**	**Hands**

What color is it?

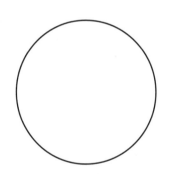	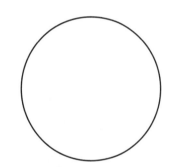	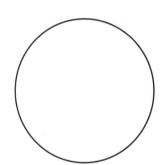
Red	**Yellow**	**Green**

  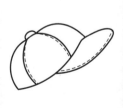 

Sorting Objects

Writing a Sentence

Introduction

Explain that a complete sentence has two parts. The subject tells who or what, and the predicate tells what action is performed. Write a subject such as *The cat* on the board. Explain that this is not a complete sentence because it gives the subject and not what the cat is doing. Have a student complete the sentence. Some possible answers may include *The cat is meowing* or *The cat is hungry*. Repeat the activity using incomplete sentences with missing subjects or predicates.

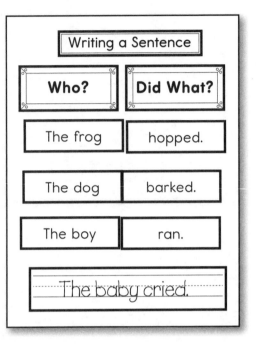

Creating the Notebook Page

Guide students through the following steps to complete the right-hand page in their notebooks.

1. Add a Table of Contents entry for the Writing a Sentence pages.

2. Cut out the title and glue it to the top of the page.

3. Cut out the labels. Glue them to the top of the page to create two columns.

4. Cut out the sentence part pieces. Read each one and decide which sentence parts go together to form complete sentences. Glue the sentences together under the correct labels.

5. Write a sentence on the blank card and glue it to the bottom of the page.

Reflect on Learning

To complete the left-hand page, have students write two more complete sentences and illustrate them. Allow time for students to share their work.

Writing a Sentence

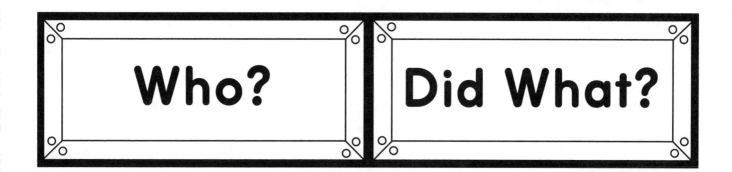

Who?	Did What?
The dog	hopped.
The frog	ran.
The boy	barked.

Using Capital Letters

Write a simple sentence on the board using a lowercase letter for the beginning of the sentence. Ask students if they notice anything wrong with the sentence. Explain that sentences begin with a capital or uppercase letter. Have a volunteer to come to the board and correct the sentence. Explain that some words called proper nouns are also capitalized. Discuss how the pronoun *I* is always capitalized. Ask students to look around the room for words that begin with capital letters. Write them on the board as students find them.

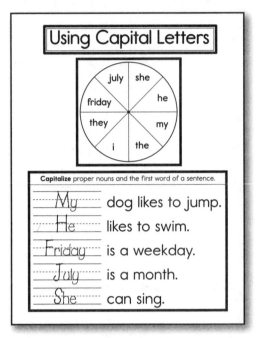

Creating the Notebook Page

Guide students through the following steps to complete the right-hand page in their notebooks.

1. Add a Table of Contents entry for the Using Capital Letters pages.

2. Cut out the title and glue it to the top of the page.

3. Cut out the spinner and glue it below the title.

4. Cut out the *Capitalize* card and glue it to the bottom of the page.

5. Use a sharpened pencil and a paper clip to spin the spinner. Use the word that is spun in a sentence using the correct capitalization. For example, if *july* is landed on, capitalize the word and write it in the *is a month* blank. Continue spinning until the chart is filled.

Reflect on Learning

To complete the left-hand page, send students on a capital letter scavenger hunt. Have students look around the room to find words that begin with capital letters. Students should record their findings in their notebooks and circle the uppercase letters in each word.

Using Capital Letters

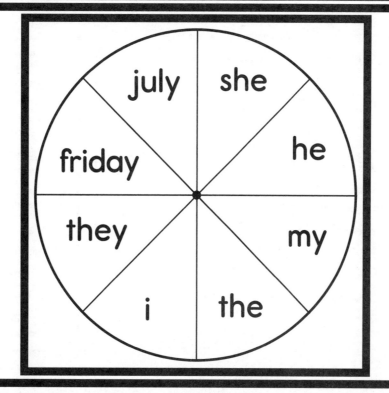

Capitalize proper nouns and the first word of a sentence.

_____ dog likes to jump.

_____ likes to swim.

_____ is a weekday.

_____ is a month.

_____ can sing.

Ending Punctuation

Introduction

Explain that every sentence ends with a punctuation mark. Draw a period, an exclamation point, and a question mark on the board. Explain that different punctuation marks are used for different types of sentences. Write a variety of simple sentences on the board, leaving off the punctuation marks. Have volunteers to come to the board, read the sentences, and place the correct punctuation mark at the end of each sentence.

Creating the Notebook Page

Guide students through the following steps to complete the right-hand page in their notebooks.

1. Add a Table of Contents entry for the Ending Punctuation pages.

2. Cut out the title and glue it to the top of the page.

3. Cut out the flap book. Cut on the solid lines to create three flaps. Apply glue to the back of the left section and attach it below the title.

4. Write a sentence using each type of punctutation mark under the flaps.

5. Cut out the sentences card. Glue it to the bottom of the page. Read each sentence. Then, write the correct punctuation mark at the end of each sentence.

6. Practice reading the sentences aloud with a partner.

Reflect on Learning

To complete the left-hand page, have each student draw a picture of something she likes to do after school. Then, each student should write a sentence about the picture and use the correct ending punctuation.

Ending Punctuation

A **punctuation mark** belongs at the **end** of a sentence.

Statement	.
Feeling	!
Question	?

I have a brown dog ☐

Do you like to read ☐

The party was fun ☐

I can run fast ☐

Do you like school ☐

Parts of a Book

Introduction

Explain the parts of a book by showing several examples of different books. Ask students what all of the books have in common. Possible answers include that all of the books have a spine, front cover, back cover, author, illustrator, and pages. Demonstrate how to hold a book properly and how to read the pages from left to right. Explain the job of the author and illustrator. Discuss the different types of books such as picture books, chapter books, dictionaries, and textbooks.

Creating the Notebook Page

Guide students through the following steps to complete the right-hand page in their notebooks.

1. Add a Table of Contents entry for the Parts of a Book pages.

2. Cut out the title and glue it to the top of the page.

3. Cut out the diagram and glue it to the center of the page.

4. Cut out the label cards. Glue each label to the correct place on the diagram.

Reflect on Learning

To complete the left-hand page, have each student draw a large rectangle. Display a copy of a book the class has read. Write the title, author, and illustrator of the book on the board. Have students copy the information in their rectangles. Then, have them draw pictures to illustrate the subject of the book.

Colorful
Fish

by Ryan Nez

Illustrated by Sara Shaw

author

back
cover

front
cover

illustrator

pages

spine

title

Parts of a Book

Main Topic and Details

Introduction

Explain that a topic is the main idea of a text, and the details tell more about the topic. Say words such as *elephants*, *monkeys*, *tigers*, and *lions* and ask students what the topic might be. A possible answer might be *the zoo*. Write a topic on the board such as *the beach*. Have volunteers provide details about the topic. Possible answers may include *seashells*, *lifeguards*, and *sand*. List the answers as students give them. Repeat this activity with another topic.

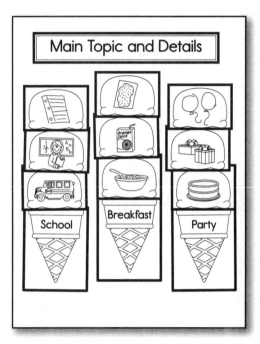

Creating the Notebook Page

Guide students through the following steps to complete the right-hand page in their notebooks.

1. Add a Table of Contents entry for the Main Topic and Details pages.

2. Cut out the title and glue it to the top of the page.

3. Cut out the ice-cream cone cards (topics). Glue them along the bottom of the page, leaving enough room to glue three scoops of ice cream (details) above each cone.

4. Cut out the ice cream cards. Look at the picture on each card to match the detail to the topic. Glue the scoops above the correct cones.

5. Draw one more detail for each topic on a blank scoop and glue it above the correct ice-cream cone.

Reflect on Learning

To complete the left-hand page, write a topic on the board such as *My favorite thing to do in the summer*. Have students draw pictures showing as many details as possible. Allow time for students to share their work.

Main Topic and Details

Setting

Introduction

Explain that every story takes place in one or more settings. It is where the action occurs. Display a familiar book such as *Goldilocks and the Three Bears*. Ask students if they know where the story takes place. Then, read the story aloud. Discuss words and phrases from the story that describe the setting.

Creating the Notebook Page

Guide students through the following steps to complete the right-hand page in their notebooks.

1. Add a Table of Contents entry for the Setting pages.

2. Cut out the title and glue it to the top of the page.

3. Cut out the flap book. Cut on the solid lines to create three flaps. Apply glue to the back of the left section and attach it to the page.

4. Read the story on each flap. Decide where the story takes place.

5. Draw a picture of the setting for each story under the flaps.

Reflect on Learning

To complete the left-hand page, have each student draw a picture of the setting from his favorite book. Allow time for students to share their work and explain why the settings are their favorites.

Setting

The **setting** is where a story takes place.

The big squirrel chased the little squirrel. They ran up and down the trees. The little squirrel hid behind a bush.

Noah's mom took Noah to a pumpkin patch. They looked at many pumpkins. They each picked a pumpkin to bring home.

Becca takes swim lessons. Her teacher is a lifeguard. Becca likes to swim under water.

Characters

Introduction

Introduce characters in a story by acting out a character from a popular story such as *The Three Little Pigs*. Encourage students to guess which character you are. Then, have a volunteer act out a different character while the other students try to guess which one it is. Explain how a character can be a person, an animal, or a thing. Discuss different character traits such as how a character looks or feels.

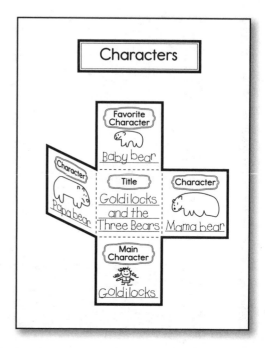

Creating the Notebook Page

Guide students through the following steps to complete the right-hand page in their notebooks.

1. Add a Table of Contents entry for the Characters pages.

2. Cut out the title and glue it to the top of the page.

3. Cut out the four-flap character square. Cut on the solid lines to create four flaps. Apply glue to the back of the center section and attach it to the page.

4. Read a book or listen to a story.

5. Draw pictures of and write the names of the main character, other characters, and a favorite character on the flaps.

6. Write a word that describes the character under each flap.

Reflect on Learning

To complete the left-hand page, have each student draw all of the characters from her favorite story. Allow time for students to describe the characters to the class.

Characters

Favorite Character

Character

Title

Character

Main Character

Sequencing Events

Explain that the word *sequence* means *order*. The sequence of events is the order in which things happen. Use the words *first*, *next*, *then*, and *last to* discuss how a person brushes his teeth. Describe how the steps have to occur in order to get the teeth cleaned properly. Compare this to reading a book. The book will not make sense unless the events occur in order.

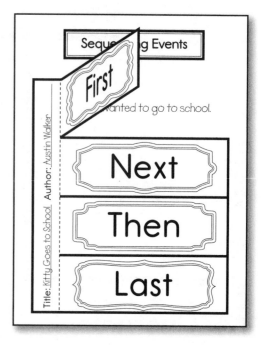

Creating the Notebook Page

Guide students through the following steps to complete the right-hand page in their notebooks.

1. Add a Table of Contents entry for the Sequencing Events pages.

2. Cut out the title and glue it to the top of the page.

3. Cut out the flap book. Cut on the solid lines to create four flaps. Apply glue to the back of the left section and attach it to the page.

4. Read or listen to a story.

5. Write the title of the story and the author on the flap book.

6. Draw pictures of or write the order of events in the story under the correct flaps.

7. Use the flap book to retell the story to a partner.

Reflect on Learning

To complete the left-hand page, have students divide their notebook pages into fourths. Label the sections *First, Next, Then,* and *Last*. Ask students to think about the order in which they brush their teeth. Have them draw pictures for each step. Allow time for students to share their work.

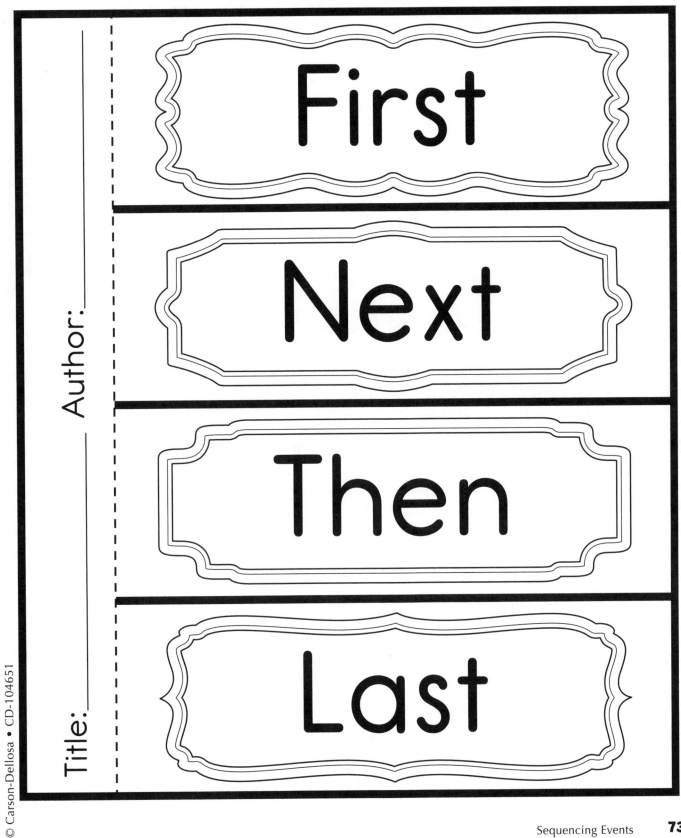

Author:

Title:

First

Next

Then

Last

Picture Predictions

Introduction

Explain that a prediction is guess about what will happen next. Discuss how a weather person looks at pictures of clouds from a weather satellite and can predict what the weather will be. Explain how looking at pictures from the story can help readers think about what might happen next. Discuss how making predictions helps readers better understand what they are reading.

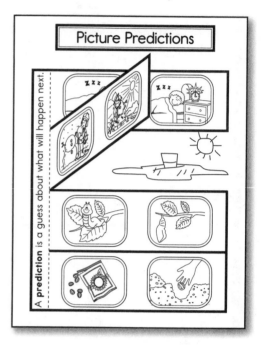

Creating the Notebook Page

Guide students through the following steps to complete the right-hand page in their notebooks.

1. Add a Table of Contents entry for the Picture Predictions pages.

2. Cut out the title and glue it to the top of the page.

3. Cut out the flap book. Cut on the solid lines to create four flaps. Apply glue to the back of the left section and attach it to the page.

4. Look at the two pictures on each flap. Write or draw a picture of a prediction of what might happen next under each flap.

Reflect on Learning

To complete the left-hand page, give each student a picture from a newspaper or magazine that shows action. Have students glue the pictures into their notebooks. Then, ask students to write or draw a picture of what they predict might happen next.

74

Picture Predictions

A **prediction** is a guess about what will happen next.

Fiction and Nonfiction

Introduction

Display pairs of fiction and nonfiction books such as *The Very Hungry Caterpillar* by Eric Carle (Philomel Books, 1994) and a book about the lifecycle of a butterfly. Discuss the various elements of fiction and nonfiction. For example, explain how a nonfiction text contains facts, real illustrations and photographs, while fiction contains make-believe stories, often with talking animals as main characters.

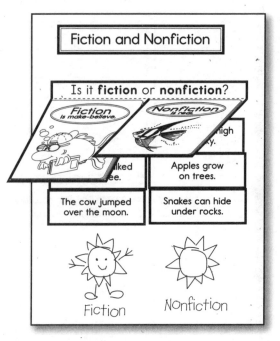

Creating the Notebook Page

Guide students through the following steps to complete the right-hand page in their notebooks.

1. Add a Table of Contents entry for the Fiction and Nonfiction pages.

2. Cut out the title and glue it to the top of the page.

3. Cut out the flap book. Cut on the solid lines to create two flaps. Apply glue to the back of the top section and attach it below the title.

4. Cut out the sentence cards. Read each sentence. Decide if the sentence belongs in a fiction book or a nonfiction book. Glue the sentence card under the correct flap.

5. On the bottom of the page, draw a picture of an object that is real and and an object that is make-believe. Label the pictures *Fiction* and *Nonfiction*.

Reflect on Learning

To complete the left-hand page, provide students with access to the classroom library. Have each student choose a fiction and a nonfiction book. With a partner, have students explain how they know they have a fiction and a nonfiction book. Students should draw objects or characters from each of their books and label them *fiction* and *nonfiction*.